NEW ROCHELLE PUBLIC LIBRARY

Everyday Materials

P9-DOB-963

Paper Products

Andrew Langley

Crabtree Publishing Company

www.crabtreebooks.com

OCT 2009

Crabtree Publishing Company
www.crabtreebooks.com

All rights reserved.
Author: Andrew Langley
Editors: Annabel Savery, Adrianna Morganelli
Proofreaders: Michael Hodge, Crystal Sikkens
Project editor: Robert Walker
Designer: Ian Winton
Illustrator: Ian Winton
Picture researcher: Rachel Tisdale
Production coordinator: Margaret Amy Salter
Prepress technician: Margaret Amy Salter

© 2009 Crabtree Publishing Company

Acknowledgements: Corbis: 12 (Sally A Morgan; Ecoscene).
Discovery Picture Library: 1, 19, and 21 (Chris Fairclough).
GettyImages: Cover (Garry Gay), 5 (Dorling Kindersley),
8 (Dr Dennis Kunkel). Istockphoto: cover and spread head
panel, 4 (Carmen Martinez), 6 (Susan Trigg), 7, 9 (Viktor
Balabanov), 10 (Max Blain), 10 lower, 14 (Natalia
Tkachenko), 15 (Rob Cruse), 16 (Yusuf Anil Akduyga), 17,
20 (Olga Shelego). M-Real: 13 and 18. Science Photo Library:
11 (David R Frazier).

Library and Archives Canada Cataloguing in Publication

Langley, Andrew
    Paper products / Andrew Langley.

(Everyday materials)
Includes index.
ISBN 978-0-7787-4128-2 (bound).--ISBN 978-0-7787-4135-0 (pbk.)

    1. Paper products--Juvenile literature. 2. Paper--Juvenile literature.
3. Papermaking--Juvenile literature. I. Title. II. Series: Langley, Andrew.
Everyday materials.

TS1105.5.L35 2008   j676   C2008-903570-4

Library of Congress Cataloging-in-Publication Data

Langley, Andrew.
  Paper products / Andrew Langley.
    p. cm. -- (Everyday materials)
  Includes index.
  ISBN-13: 978-0-7787-4135-0 (pbk. : alk. paper)
  ISBN-10: 0-7787-4135-4 (pbk. : alk. paper)
  ISBN-13: 978-0-7787-4128-2 (reinforced library binding : alk. paper)
  ISBN-10: 0-7787-4128-1 (reinforced library binding : alk. paper)
  1. Paper--Juvenile literature. 2. Papermaking--Juvenile literature. I. Title. II. Series.

TS1105.5.L36 2008
676'.28--dc22

                    2008024011

Crabtree Publishing Company
www.crabtreebooks.com   1-800-387-7650

Copyright © **2009 CRABTREE PUBLISHING COMPANY**. All rights reserved. No
part of this publication may be reproduced, stored in a retrieval system or be transmitted in
any form or by any means, electronic, mechanical, photocopying, recording, or otherwise,
without the prior written permission of Crabtree Publishing Company.

Published in Canada
Crabtree Publishing
616 Welland Ave.
St. Catharines, Ontario
L2M 5V6

Published in the United States
Crabtree Publishing
PMB16A
350 Fifth Ave., Suite 3308
New York, NY 10118

First published in 2008
by Wayland
338 Euston Road
London NW1 3BH

Wayland Australia
Level 17/207 Kent Street
Sydney, NSW 2000

Copyright © Wayland 2008

Contents

What is paper?

There is paper everywhere. We read newspapers and books made of paper. We use paper napkins, bags, and envelopes.

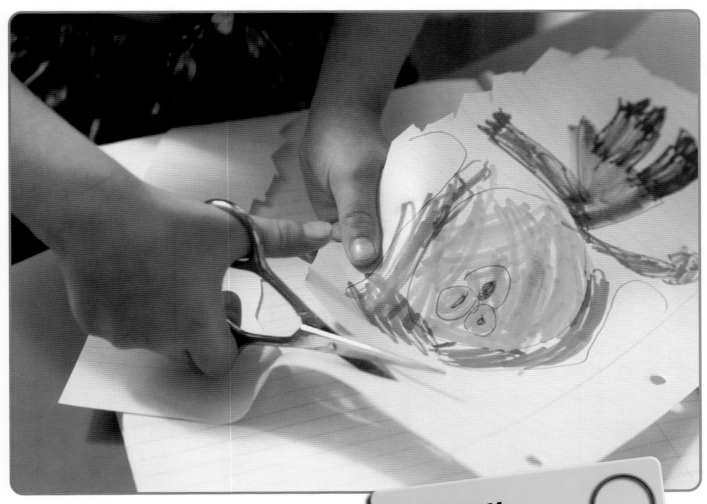

Paper can be used in many different ways. It is light and thin. It is also easy to bend and cut.

Eye spy

Look around your classroom. How many things are made of paper?

5

Different kinds of paper

There are thousands of different kinds of paper. Thinnest of all is **tissue paper**, which is very soft. Paper for books is thicker.

Eye spy

Find five kinds of **cardboard** in your home.

Brown wrapping paper is used for bags and **packaging**. Cardboard is thicker and stronger than paper is. It is made of several layers of paper.

Cardboard is used to make boxes.

What is paper made of?

Paper is made of millions of tiny hairs. These are called **fibers**. They are tangled together to form a stiff mat of paper.

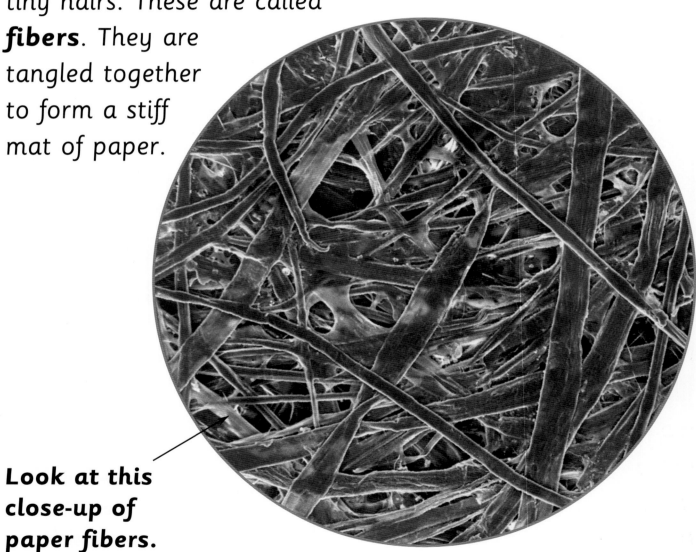

Look at this close-up of paper fibers.

We can also make paper from straw.

Nearly all paper fibers come from wood. Other materials are also used, such as **cotton**, **linen** and **straw**.

What do you think?

It is easy to tear one sheet of newspaper. Now try tearing a whole newspaper. Why is it so difficult?

The pulp mill

Logs of wood arrive at the **pulp mill**. A machine breaks them up into small chips. The chips are mixed with water and chemicals.

The mixture is heated in a big tank. The wood fibers become soft. The mixture turns into a mushy liquid called **pulp**.

Did you know?

White paper is made by adding **bleach** to the pulp. The bleach takes away all other colors.

Rolling and drying

The wet pulp comes out of the tank and is spread on **wire mesh**. Huge rollers squeeze the water out of the pulp. The water drains away through the holes in the wire mesh.

When the paper is dry, it is rolled into huge rolls.

Eye spy

Can you find any paper on a roll in your home?

13

Treating paper

We can color paper by adding **dyes** to the pulp. Paper for books is also **coated** with **size**. This is a glue that stops the ink from spreading over the paper.

Cups and cartons have a covering of wax or plastic. This stops liquid from soaking through the paper.

What do you think?

Which kind of paper soaks up water best — newspaper or shiny magazine paper?

15

Special uses

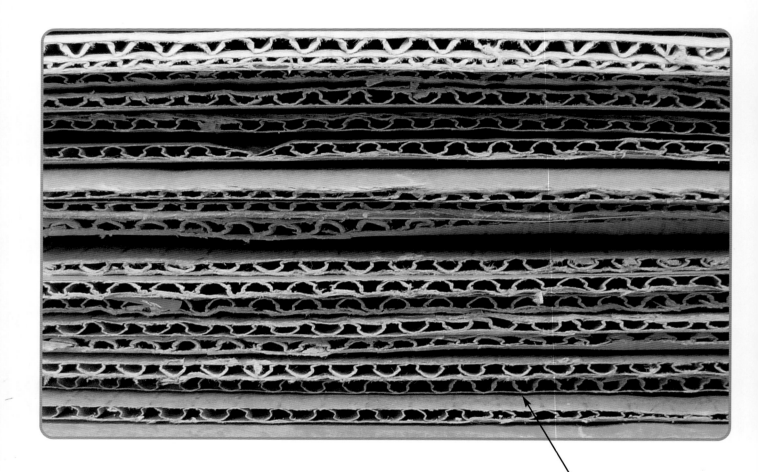

Corrugated board is even stronger than cardboard. It has three layers, like a sandwich. The middle layer of paper is shaped into folds.

Folded inner layer

We use paper in some surprising places. Car engines have paper **filters**. The filters keep the oil and air clean.

Did you know?

Paper was first made in China, nearly 2000 years ago.

Paper is also used to make the face masks that surgeons wear.

Recycling paper

It takes a lot of wood to make paper. Most of this comes from new forests. The trees are planted to supply the pulp mills.

But old paper can be used again. The fibers in the paper can be turned to pulp and made into new paper.

Eye spy

Do you have a recycling bin at home? Do you put old newspapers into it?

Quiz

Questions

1. What is most paper made of?
2. What happens in a pulp mill?
3. How is the water squeezed out of the pulp?
4. What does bleach do?
5. What happens to wood fibers when they get wet?

Answers

5. Wood fibers go soft when they get wet.
4. Bleach takes the color out of wood pulp.
3. Big rollers squeeze the water out of the pulp.
2. The wood is broken into chips and turned into pulp.
1. Most paper is made of wood.

Paper topic web

Geography
If you want to write to someone in another country, you can buy special airmail paper. This paper is very light.

Art and design
You can make things with papier-mâché. This is mashed up paper mixed with glue. It can be molded into shapes and decorated.

History
Ancient Egyptians used parts of plants to make their own paper-like materials.

Science
A type of paper called litmus paper changes color in different liquids. Ask your science teacher to show you.

English
All the books you read are printed on paper. Read "The Paper Bag Princess" by Robert Munsch. She has to wear a paper bag when a dragon burns all her clothes!

Glossary

bleach The chemical that removes the color from materials

cardboard A strong kind of paper made from layers of pulp

coated Covered with a thin layer of something

corrugated Folded into a series of ridges or grooves

cotton Cloth made from the fibers of the cotton plant

dye Something that gives color to a material

fibers The tiny, hair-like strands that make up trees and other plants

filter A very fine mesh, or something with small holes that stops dirt from passing through it

linen Cloth made from the fibers of the flax plant

packaging Paper, cardboard, and other materials used to wrap up food and other products

pulp A mixture of wood fibers, water, and chemicals

pulp mill A place where wood is mixed with water and turned into a soggy mixture called pulp

size A kind of glue used to coat paper

straw The stalks of wheat and other grain crops

tissue paper A fine, soft, and thin kind of paper

wire mesh A flat net made of crossed metal wires

Further information

Books to read

Amazing Science: Materials. Sally Hewitt. Wayland, 2006.

Science Explorers: Paper: Exploring the Science of Everyday Materials.
Nicola Edwards and Jane Harris. A & C Black Publishers, 2003.

Raintree Perspectives: Using Materials: How We Use Paper. Chris Oxlade. Raintree
Publishers, 2004.

Start-Up Science: Materials. Claire Llewellyn. Evans Brothers Ltd., 2004.

Web sites to visit

Paper University
http://www.tappi.org/paperu/welcome.htm
Click on the Fun & Games link to play exciting paper games!

Confederation of Paper Industries Kids Korna
http://www.paper.org.uk/info/kids/homemade.htm
Learn how to make your own paper here.

Recycling guide
http://www.recycling-guide.org.uk/paper.html
Learn all about how paper is recycled.

Index

Printed in China